Learn to Paint

MIXED MEDIA

Moira Huntly

HarperCollins*Publishers*

First published in 1992
by HarperCollins Publishers
London
Reprinted 1993

© Moira Huntly 1992

Moira Huntly asserts the moral right to be
identified as the author of this work

Editor: Patsy North
Art Editor: Caroline Hill
Designer: Paul Griffin
Photographer: Ed Barber

The painting on this page is *Staithes, Yorkshire*,
watercolour and gouache 38.5 × 75 cm (15⅛ × 29½ in)

**A catalogue record for this book is available from
the British Library**

ISBN 0 00 412618 1

Printed and bound in Hong Kong

CONTENTS

PORTRAIT OF AN ARTIST
MOIRA HUNTLY

Fig. 1　Moira Huntly at work in her studio

Born in Scotland, Moira Huntly spent her early childhood in Northern Spain, until the outbreak of the Spanish Civil War. Forced to escape, Moira and her family were rescued by a British naval escort and became refugees in Portugal for a while, eventually making a safe passage to Britain. The family moved to the Wirral in Cheshire, and later to London, where Moira studied for five years at Harrow School of Art and a further year at Hornsey College of Art. She received a thorough and disciplined grounding in drawing and painting, and gained a London University degree in art teaching.

Moira Huntly first became interested in mixed media painting when preparing her degree thesis during her period at art school. Her research made her aware that many artists have worked with more than one medium at a time, and that there is nothing new in the idea of painting in mixed media. She herself paints with traditional materials, sometimes in unexpected combinations. She applies them in an imaginative way, looking for abstract pattern and design in subjects, but mostly portraying them with a certain amount of twentieth century realism. Subjects that interest Moira are wide-ranging, from marine and architectural images to figures, still life, industrial landscapes and complicated machinery. Her work is continually developing, and her ideas are expressed with strength and vitality in a painterly way, in which

Fig. 2 Working with printing ink and pastels

her ability and love of drawing are very evident.

Moira Huntly was elected to the Pastel Society in 1978 and to the Royal Institute of Painters in Watercolours in 1981, and she serves on the Council of both societies. In 1985 she was winner of the Winsor and Newton Prize for the best group of paintings at the Royal Institute's Annual Exhibition, and in the same year she was elected to the Royal Society of Marine Artists, where she now also serves on the Council. In 1986 she was winner of the Laing National Painting Competition.

Moira contributes to various art magazines and is the author of several books on drawing and painting. Her first books – *Draw Still Life*, *Draw Nature* and *Draw with Brush and Ink* – were part of a series, and she is also author of *Imaginative Still Life*, *Painting and Drawing Boats* and for HarperCollins, *Painting in Mixed Media* and *Learn to Paint Gouache*.

At present Moira lives in the Cotswold village of Willersey, where she brought up her family, and she has studio in Stow-on-the-Wold, Gloucestershire. She exhibits regularly at the Mall Galleries in London, as well as in a few selected galleries and museums in Britain, North America and Germany. Her paintings are in many collections worldwide and she regularly undertakes important commissions internationally.

THE EXCITEMENT OF MIXED MEDIA

Every day of the week I am either painting or drawing, thinking or writing about painting, and there are times when I get stale and inspiration, even the desire to paint, deserts me for a while. Sometimes I escape from this impasse by experimenting with different media, and I often make an unexpected discovery which revives my painting energy.

In this book I suggest just a few of the many possible combinations of media, nearly all of which have been employed by painters in the past and have therefore stood the test of time. The only rules to be observed are practical ones, as every medium has its limitations and not every medium is technically compatible with another. Each section of the book deals with a different combination of media and explains a few basic techniques, followed by some exercises or a demonstration painting.

Whenever I visit exhibitions I notice that paintings which bear the description 'mixed media' immediately create an interest. Recently I visited the Burrell Collection in Glasgow, where I was able to look closely at the paintings of Degas and Toulouse

Fig. 3 *Still Life with Red Curtain*, Indian ink and oil pastel, 16.5 × 20.5 cm (6½ × 8 in)

6

Fig. 4 *Still Life with Violins*, watercolour and soft pastel, 53.5 × 74 cm (21 × 29 in)

Lautrec and see at first hand how boldly they had mixed their media. It was a revelation to realize that there is nothing new about the idea of combining different media within a single work. Medieval illustrators produced beautifully worked images with watercolour, gouache and gold leaf. Leonardo da Vinci made many drawings with chalks and silver point (a silver wire held in wood, later replaced by graphite pencils) on prepared coloured gesso grounds, and he is reputed to have invented pastel.

More recently, we are familiar with the work of the cubists who combined chalk and gouache with oil on cardboard; oil, pastel and paper collage on board; and many other variations. John Piper's evocative paintings of the British Isles have been perfectly depicted with mixed media, using combinations of watercolour, ink, wax and gouache to describe ancient buildings and wild romantic landscapes. From many examples such as these, we can see that working with mixed media is a valid technique if it helps to give us greater versatility in creating the images we wish to convey.

The scope of mixed media and the choice of materials are so wide that it might seem confusing at first. It is best to begin by choosing materials with which you are familiar. The support is important and the media you are using must be technically compatible, so find out the limitations. For example, as oil repels water,

acrylic can only be applied to a grease-free surface and therefore will not work well if painted on top of oil paint. Oil paint, however, can be worked on top of acrylic. The characteristics of some media lend themselves to a particular way of working: for example, pen and ink can be a means of producing fine detail, whereas oil pastels make much broader marks. Combining such media widens the scope of the images we can create within a single painting.

My painting, *Still Life with Red Curtain* (**fig. 3**), combines Indian ink and oil pastel and shows the colour vitality of which oil pastel is capable, the subtlety of pastel worked over Indian ink, and graffito techniques which reveal the inked undersurface. For the other still-life painting of violins (**fig. 4**), I chose watercolour and soft pastel, and the support was vivid orange pastel paper which strongly influenced the painting. In places I left it uncovered, in other places it shows through thin layers of watercolour and pastel. In some areas, intense layers of pastel were applied.

It is exciting to experiment with as many media as possible to discover which are most suited to your style of painting. Do not be afraid of failures – they form part of our progress and he who ventures nothing, gains nothing. There is no end to our development as painters – it is a continuous process of exploration and it is ideas that count, techniques only providing the means of expression.

7

WHAT EQUIPMENT DO YOU NEED?

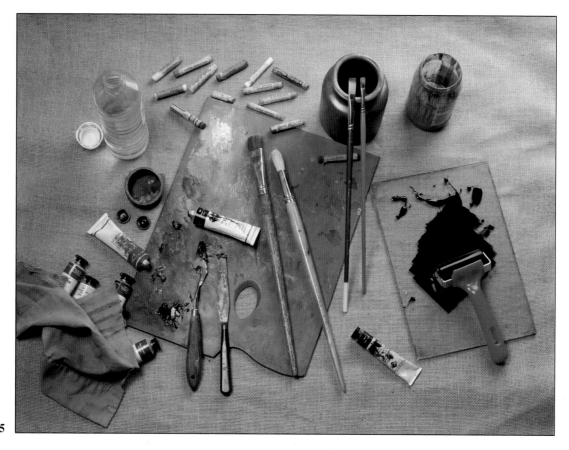

Fig. 5

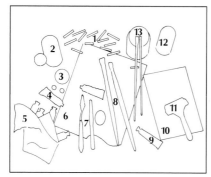

Oil-based media and equipment

1	Oil pastels	9	Black block printing ink
2	Turpentine	10	Glass slab
3	Dipper	11	64 mm (2½ in) printing
4	Oil paints		roller
5	Rag	12	Turps jar for cleaning
6	Wooden oil palette		brushes
7	Palette knives	13	Brush holder
8	Hog bristle oil brushes:		
	25 mm (1 in), Nos. 10, 5, 3		

It can be bewildering to go into an art shop to be confronted with a wide variety of brushes and pigments and not know what to choose, so the purpose of this section is to give some guide-lines, and to list the materials I have used throughout the book. I am not suggesting, however, that you should go out and purchase everything at once. In fact, many of the colours that I have chosen are optional and you can substitute your own choice if you prefer.

It is wise to start with basic materials that you are familiar with and gradually add to these as you become more experimental. You will find it rewarding to work with good-quality materials if you can afford them; it is better to have a few good products than a large quantity of inferior ones.

Oil-based media

In addition to oil paint, I have included oil pastel and oil-based printing ink. My choice of oil paint was simple – three warm and three cool colours, but I used a wider range of oil pastels, including gold. All these media require turpentine for thinning the pigment and also for cleaning purposes, along with plenty of rags.

Oil paint Cadmium Yellow, Raw Umber, Mars Red, Cobalt Blue, Viridian, Lamp Black.

Oil pastel Lemon Yellow, Yellow Ochre, White, Orange, Burnt Sienna, Pink, Olive Green, Prussian Blue, Ultramarine Blue, Light Grey, Dark Grey, Payne's Grey and Gold.

Daler-Rowney oil-based Block Printing Colour Black.

Other equipment A printing roller No. 0, 64 mm (2½ in); a glass or plastic slab; an oil palette (wooden, plastic or tear-off paper); a palette knife; turpentine.

Drawing media

Soft pastel Warm Grey, Cool Grey, Blue Grey, Purple Grey, Green Grey, Grass Green, Olive Green, Yellow Ochre, Raw Sienna, Burnt Umber, Purple Brown, Coeruleum, Rose Madder, Poppy Red, Crimson Lake, Pansy Violet, French Ultramarine.

Soft pastel is included here because it is a dry medium, but is it also a medium that allows you to paint as well as draw, and the colours can be brilliant and scintillating. Daler Rowney produce over 50 colours, each of which has a tint range from 0 (the palest) up to 6 or 8 (the darkest), and I choose pastels from this vast selection as I need them. Any paintings that include pastel will remain permanent and fresh if protected behind glass.

Pastel pencils Sanguine, Olive Green, Grey, Black, White.

Square pastels

Pastel pencils and square pastels are harder than soft pastels, enabling you to make finer lines for details.

Wax crayons Yellow, Orange, Green, Blue.

Other drawing media Willow charcoal; charcoal pencil; black drawing pencil; Kandahar Black Indian ink; dip pen; black fine-line waterproof pen; felt-tipped pen; twig; white candle.

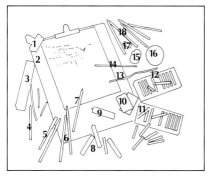

Drawing materials and equipment

1	Bulldog clip	10	Putty rubber
2	Drawing board	11	Soft pastels
3	Charcoal sticks	12	Square pastels
4	Charcoal pencil	13	Twig
5	Black fine-line pen	14	Dip pen
6	Felt-tipped pens	15	Black Indian ink
7	Black drawing pencil	16	Pot
8	Wax crayons	17	Razor blade
9	Wax candle	18	Pastel pencils

Fig. 6

Fig. 7

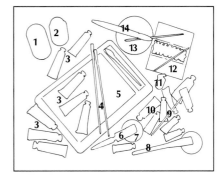

Water-based media and equipment

1 Water jar	7 China stacking palettes
2 Acrylic Texture Paste	8 Wash brush
3 Acrylic colour	9 Sable brush
4 Hog bristle brushes for	10 Gouache
acrylics	11 White poster paint
5 'Stay-Wet' palette for	12 Watercolour box
acrylics	13 Saucer
6 38 mm (1½ in) house	14 Watercolour brushes
painter's brush	

Water-based media

Watercolour Cadmium Yellow, Raw Sienna, Yellow Ochre, Cadmium Orange, Cadmium Red, Crimson Alizarin, Burnt Sienna, Brown Madder, Prussian Blue, Cobalt Blue, French Ultramarine, Hooker's Green, Olive Green, Burnt Umber and Lamp Black.

I personally prefer to use Artists' quality transparent watercolour, but student-quality tubes are perfectly adequate.

Acrylic Cadmium Yellow Pale, Lemon Yellow, Burnt Sienna, Rowney Orange, Raw Umber, Hooker's Green, Monestial Blue, Ultramarine, Payne's Grey, Titanium White.

Acrylic is a medium which gives instant results because of its fast drying time. Used thickly, it gives a consistency more like oil paint, whereas, thinned with water, it can be used transparently in a similar way to watercolour. It can also be mixed with Acrylic

Texture Paste to build up impasto. You can paint on any support, but do not mix with oil or paint on an oil-based ground. Try to keep brushes in water during the painting session.

Gouache Lemon Yellow, Brilliant Yellow, Yellow Ochre, Raw Sienna, Middle Orange, Raw Umber, Cadmium Red, Ultramarine, Delft Blue, Olive Green, Cool Grey 1, Neutral Grey, Permanent White.

This is also known as body colour and is an opaque watercolour which combines well with other media. It dries quickly, can be diluted and applied in thin washes like watercolour, or applied more thickly to look like oil paint.

Poster colour White.

Palettes A selection of palettes is useful for water-based media: china or plastic saucers for watercolour or gouache; an easy-to-clean plastic palette, a throw-away paper palette or a 'Stay-Wet' palette for acrylics.

Brushes

You can achieve a wide variety of effects with the following range of brushes: No. 000, No. 5 and No. 7 round Kolinsky sables; Series 66 squirrel/goat hair extra-large round wash brush; Series D22 25 mm (1 in) flat Dalon wash brush; 38 mm (1½ in) house painter's brush; Series B48 Bristlewhite long flat hog bristle brushes No. 3 and No. 5; Series 115 long filbert hog bristle brush No. 10.

Supports

The support is a very important factor in all painting, providing a variety of surface textures. I have listed here the supports used throughout the book, but you could try many of the techniques on different papers and boards, and assess the resulting quality of line or brush marks.

Supports (**fig. 8**): Cartridge paper; Ingres paper; Canson pastel paper; Canson card, 300 gsm (140 lb); Bockingford watercolour paper NOT, 300 gsm (140 lb) and 638 gsm (300 lb); Saunders Waterford paper NOT, 300 gsm (140 lb); Whatman HP, 300 gsm (140 lb); Daler Line and Wash board; Studland mounting board; canvas board.

Fig. 8

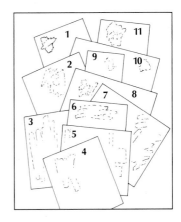

Supports

1 Mounting board with ink and oil pastel
2 Cartridge paper with watercolour and candlewax
3 Whatman HP 300 gsm (140 lb) with oil paint and turpentine
4 Bockingford watercolour paper NOT 300 gsm (140 lb) with gouache and pastel pencils
5 Ingres paper with printing ink
6 Saunders Waterford watercolour paper NOT 300 gsm (140 lb) with watercolour
7 Canvas board with oil paint and soft pastel
8 Canson pastel paper with soft pastel
9 Canson card with Indian ink
10 Canson pastel paper with gouache
11 Daler Line and Wash Board with acrylic wash and gold oil pastel

WATERCOLOUR AND WAX

I have chosen to start with a mixed media idea which does not require any complicated equipment, but simply uses watercolour, candle wax and white paper. The idea is based on the fact that wax will repel water, acting as a resist, and those of you who have practised the art of batik will be familiar with this technique.

I like to think of these first exercises as magic painting doodles. They are fun to do, and the magic part occurs when watercolour is brushed over an invisible candle wax doodle which then miraculously appears as a white pattern.

In **fig. 9** I drew a curly pattern on smooth white cartridge paper, pressing down firmly with the end of a white candle. Although the wax is colourless, it is shiny, and if you look along the surface of the paper at eye level, you can see where wax has been applied. Then I washed Cadmium Orange watercolour over the wax with a No. 7 soft watercolour brush and the pattern was revealed.

When the orange wash was completely dry more candle wax was applied over part of this wash, again pressing firmly so that a good layer of wax was deposited. Crimson Alizarin was brushed over the paper (**fig. 10**), revealing the masked areas on the orange wash and retaining the first waxing as white paper. Globules of paint often adhere unevenly to the wax, giving a pleasing textural effect.

On the pattern of bricks in **fig. 11**, the technique is taken a stage further with the introduction of a third waxing and third colour. In this case, I used French Ultramarine as the final wash, and the stronger colour brushed over crimson gave a very rich dark tone.

I have used the same three colours for this abstract image in **fig. 12**, and there the globules of paint that have adhered to the wax are very obvious where the colour is very dark in tone.

Quite complicated images and designs can be created by repeating these processes many times with successive layers of watercolour and waxings.

For **fig. 13** I have introduced coloured wax crayons on watercolour paper. As you can see here, wax tends to be distributed over the surface in an uneven broken manner on paper which has a rough texture. This doodle began with scribbles in green and orange wax crayon on the white paper, followed by a wash of dilute Prussian Blue watercolour.

Fig. 9

Fig. 10

Fig. 11

Fig. 13

Fig. 12

Watercolour, candle wax and wax crayons

For these leaf exercises I chose a smooth white paper to enable me to achieve a certain amount of definition when drawing the veins with wax. For **fig. 14** I gave the paper an all-over wash of pale Raw Sienna and when this was dry, I outlined the leaf shape with a No. 5 watercolour brush and very pale Hooker's Green. Candle wax and yellow wax crayon were scribbled over the dry background wash, and some leaf veins were drawn with yellow or green wax crayons. (It is important to allow washes to dry before crayoning so that the wax will adhere properly and the paper does not tear.) A light Prussian Blue wash was brushed all over and left to dry. Finally I painted the leaf shapes with dark mixes of Prussian Blue and Olive Green.

The effects are more subtle on the leaves in **fig. 15**. I painted the leaves with very pale French Ultramarine blue and allowed it to dry before adding white candle wax to the background. The same pale blue wash was then brushed over the background, revealing the application of wax as white paper.

In **fig. 16** I drew round the edge of the leaves with candle wax and picked out one or two of the central veins, then scribbled gently over parts of the background with green and yellow wax crayons. Some leaves were painted with Olive Green, adding a little French Ultramarine on others.

Fig. 14

Fig. 15

Fig. 16

Fig. 17   *Pembrokeshire Coast*, watercolour and wax,   25.5 × 27 cm (10 × 10¾ in)

Pembrokeshire Coast (fig. 17)   Rocks and sea-spray are ideal subjects for watercolour and wax techniques. The only wax I have used in this painting is candle wax which is quite obvious on the sea, but its use is more subtle on the rock faces. I used 300 gsm (140 lb) Bockingford watercolour paper and its strong texture helped to create some of the mottled effects, particularly on areas of frothing sea.

The subject was depicted with a brief pencil outline and no shading. I deposited a fairly thick layer of candle wax around the base of the rocks to suggest white swirling sea and spray, and then laid a light all-over wash of Prussian Blue mixed with Raw Sienna which gave a soft greeny grey. When this was dry, I added a little more Prussian Blue to the mix and painted the distant coast as a flat wash. Cool colours recede so this soft blue gave a good feeling of distance. Warm colours come forward in a painting, so for the middle distance coastline I added more Raw Sienna to the mix to give a warmer bias to the wash. The foreground rocks were painted without any blue, just Raw Sienna and Olive Green.

Patience is required to wait for all to dry before applying some candle wax over the light faces of the foreground rocks. I gave some definition to the rocks by drawing with a dip pen filled with a brushful of Burnt Umber watercolour. This watercolour pen line blends in with the rock colours. A darker wash of Burnt Umber and Olive Green was brushed over the waxed rock surfaces to give textural effects, and the sea colour was deepened in the foreground, allowing globules of paint to settle on the wax.

15

Demonstration 1: Venetian Doorway

Recently I visited Venice and spent a wonderful week drawing and painting in this unique city, discovering for myself why it acts as such a magnet to so many artists. I was particularly attracted to the architecture, with its decorative details and crumbling stonework, and decided to make a Venetian doorway the subject for this first demonstration. If you refer back to the brick wall doodle on page 13, you can see that wax is an effective medium for describing the textures of buildings and in this painting I have used blue and orange wax crayons, sometimes mixing them (fig. 18).

First stage (fig. 19) I chose a watercolour paper of medium texture and made a light pencil outline of the main features. I applied thin and thick layers of candle wax to areas that were to remain white, and then made an all-over wash of Yellow Ochre watercolour with a large brush. The watercolour must be allowed to dry completely before going on to the next stage.

Second stage (fig. 20) I drew the window grille with the end of a candle and applied more wax to parts of

Fig. 18

the stonework. Then I brushed very dilute Burnt Sienna over the wall so that the parts I had just waxed showed up as light Yellow Ochre textures. Doors and windows were then painted with a darker wash of Burnt Sienna. When the paper was dry again I drew with blue and orange wax crayons, sometimes scribbling them together over parts of the wall to make a darker texture.

Finished stage (fig. 21) I now added dilute washes of French Ultramarine and Burnt Umber over parts of the wall and finally made doors and windows darker.

Fig. 19　First stage

Fig. 20　Second stage

Fig. 21   Finished stage, *Venetian Doorway*, watercolour and wax crayons, 28 × 21 cm (11 × 8¼ in)

WATERCOLOUR AND INK

Fig. 22 *Towards Rhiconich, Sutherland*, watercolour and Indian ink, 40.5 × 51 cm (16 × 20 in)

For most of us, watercolour and ink is a familiar combination of media and, in particular, the technique of line and wash which I have chosen as the first exercise in this section. In other sections of the book you will find Indian ink combined with pastel, or with gouache, or used diluted in a wet-in-wet wash technique.

Towards Rhiconich, Sutherland (fig. 22)   Line and wash can be approached in more than one way: a pen-and-ink drawing can be added over a loose wash or a wash can be added to a pen-and-ink drawing. The sketch I made amongst the mountains of Sutherland in the northwest region of Scotland is from my sketchbook and uses the latter method. It was drawn with an Edding waterproof pen and watercolour was added to the drawing afterwards. In this case the colour was placed with a certain amount of precision in its relationship to the drawn line, and my aim was to record the subtle variations of colour to provide me with a good reference for future paintings. My main interest in this subject was the light on the water echoed by the shape of the light on the road.

Raglan   In my sketch of Raglan, I used another approach to line and wash, starting with some very loose colour washes on Hot Pressed watercolour paper. Daler Line and Wash Board is also excellent for this type of work. These washes were executed at speed and so there is a certain spontaneity about them.

This is quite a small sketch, 19 cm (7½ in) square. The washes are simple (**fig. 23**) and I used only four colours: French Ultramarine, Burnt Umber, Burnt Sienna and Olive Green. For this gentle scene Burnt Sienna and Olive Green were too fierce on their own, so I adjusted each of them with the addition of a little Burnt Umber. I superimposed the church tower over the blue sky with a wash of Burnt Umber and this colour combination resulted in a subtle stone colour.

When the washes were dry, I started drawing with a dip pen and black Indian ink (**fig. 24**), not worrying about keeping to the edges of the wash and, surprisingly, this had the effect of pulling my rather untidy washes together. Any inadvertent runs or overlaps with the watercolour washes became integrated with the pen-and-ink drawing.

18

Fig. 23

Fig. 24
Raglan, watercolour
and Indian ink,
19 × 19 cm (7½ × 7½ in)

Fig. 25 First stage

Fig. 26 Second stage

Winter Trees This little tree painting was made during a visit to North Wales where the trees seem ancient, all mossy and mottled grey like the stone walls around them.

First stage (fig. 25) The mass of branches was complicated, so for this exercise I made a light pencil outline as a guide but omitted the smallest branches.

Second stage (fig. 26)   I prepared some dilute Indian ink in a small saucer, dampened the paper with clean water and then softly brushed the ink mixture across the upper branches and over the tree trunks and stones. Using a less dilute mixture, I added darker tones onto the trunks and stones before the first wash dried. I had been working with the paper flat, but found that I could manipulate the spread of these darker ink washes if I carefully tilted the paper. **Fig. 27** shows more clearly the way ink will flare out on a wet surface and leave speckled and mottled effects when dry. Similarly you can see that a pen line drawn on damp paper will spread and become fuzzy compared to a line drawn on dry paper.

Finished stage (fig. 28)   I added subtle colour washes of Olive Green and Burnt Sienna. When these were dry, I used a dip pen and undiluted ink for details.

Fig. 27

20

Fig. 28   Finished stage, *Winter Trees*, watercolour and Indian ink, 22 × 18.5 cm (8¾ × 7¼ in)

Fig. 29 *Larch Branches*, watercolour and Indian ink, 33 × 52 cm (13 × 20½ in)

Larch Branches In the previous painting, *Winter Trees* on page 21, I used dilute Indian ink with watercolour washes. Now I am going to repeat the process in this monochrome study of larch branches and fruit **(fig. 29)**, and once again the ink is used with a wet-in-wet technique. The process of brushing ink into the watercolour washes before they dry requires some speed when working on a large painting, so prepare a small pot of diluted ink before you start.

I applied washes of Brown Madder watercolour onto heavy cartridge paper with a large round wash brush, pausing to outline the pots and fruit with the tip of the brush. I strengthened parts of this preliminary wash with more Brown Madder and then worked dilute Indian ink into the shadows. While the paper was still damp I drew the objects more carefully, using a twig dipped into ink. The quality of line is interesting: it is sharp at first, soft and blurred in very wet areas, and gives a dry brush effect as the twig gradually absorbs the ink. The larch branches were superimposed over the background washes using the twig, and here the variations in line work are more obvious. You will notice that some of the branches peter out at their tips and some of the cones are worked into as the twig becomes dry.

Fig. 30

22

Fig. 31 *Teazels*, watercolour, Indian ink and wax crayons, 30.5 × 21.5 cm (12 × 8½in)

Teazels The teazel painting is more experimental. In **fig. 30** I first dampened a sheet of 300 gsm (140 lb) watercolour paper with a spongeful of clean water, and then brushed dilute ink onto a piece of stiff scrap paper and pressed it face down onto the damp paper. Next came the exciting moment as the scrap paper was lifted off and I viewed the resulting texture, which is always unpredictable. Then a brushful of undiluted ink was dropped onto the wet paper and it flared out at the edges, giving some spidery lines which sug-gested a teazel. I expanded this idea by suggesting leaf shapes with more dilute ink.

When the surface was dry (**fig. 31**) I added branches and more teazels with a dip pen and ink, then worked white and orange wax crayons over them, and green wax crayon over the background. I applied a wash of Olive Green watercolour over the whole paper with a big brush and then washes of Burnt Umber and Pruss-ian Blue. Finally I added extra touches of yellow and white wax crayon to the teazels.

23

POSTER COLOUR RESIST AND INK

On pages 12 and 13, I called the first exercises with watercolour and wax 'magic painting doodles', because the image only becomes apparent after the colour is added. Now I am going to demonstrate another magic technique, but I must warn you that your first attempt at this process may require some nerve. It is a resist process where poster colour is used as the resist and Indian ink is painted over the whole work. The image reappears as the resist is washed off under a running tap, and this is always a nail-biting moment. Usually the finished result is surprisingly pleasing with interesting graphic qualities.

Poster paint is not a permanent medium, but it is ideal as a resist which is to be washed away. The paint covers well and has a thick consistency which, when dry, prevents the ink from penetrating through.

First stage (fig. 32)   I used a piece of card, but any thick cartridge paper would do, and I made a pencil outline of a simple boat shape. Then I decided which parts of the boat and areas of water were to be white, and painted them with thick poster paint. I have tinted my poster paint here so that it shows up in the photograph, but it is better to use white in case the paper becomes stained by a colour.

Second stage (fig. 33)   When the poster paint was quite dry, I took up a 25 mm (1 in) flat wash brush and quickly covered the whole paper with Indian ink. I then left this to dry.

Finished stage (fig. 34)   I put the paper in the sink, turned on the tap, and as the poster paint began to dissolve, it started to float off, taking the layer of Indian ink with it. I usually help this process by gently teasing the paint away with a brush or sponge. The ink remains on the unpainted parts of the paper. If you look at this stage carefully, you will notice some grey mottled areas. This happened because I was impatient and did not wait until all the ink was completely dry before washing off. I actually quite like this effect and often use it deliberately to make textures.

Boats at Staithes   The same processes took place for this painting, with some additional texture at the top left corner created by dragging poster paint with a dry brush. This allowed some ink to penetrate (**fig. 35**). Finally I added watercolour washes and some fine details to complete the image (**fig. 36**).

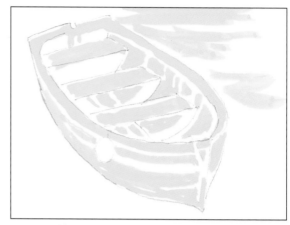

Fig. 32   **First stage**

Fig. 33   **Second stage**

Fig. 34   **Finished stage**

24

Fig. 35

Fig. 36   *Boats at Staithes*, Indian ink, poster paint resist and watercolour, 21.5 × 33 cm (8½ × 13 in)

CHARCOAL AND ACRYLIC

Fig. 37

Demonstration 2: Smethwick Canal

I enjoy translating a simple direct sketch into a mixed media painting. Sometimes the media will spontaneously suggest themselves as I view the sketch. On other occasions I purposely decide to paint with a particular combination of media and then go through my sketchbooks seeking a suitable image. This is what happened in the case of the *Smethwick Canal* sketch (**fig. 37**). I visualized a combination of thin acrylic washes contrasted with areas of thick impasto and soft charcoal textures to convey town buildings, and this canal subject seemed ideal.

A thin transparent wash of acrylic paint gives a permanent base to work on, it cannot be washed off as with watercolour, and subsequent washes do not disturb the first wash. Thick acrylic paint has covering power and can be applied with brush or palette knife in the same way as oil paint. However, a very important difference between oil paint and acrylic paint is that acrylic can be mixed with water or acrylic medium and it dries very quickly, with a matt non-greasy surface. I find that a 'Stay-Wet' palette is very useful for keeping paint moist while work progresses, and it is very important to keep brushes moist and to

wash them out thoroughly as soon as you have finished painting with them.

First stage (fig. 38) I used a very limited palette for this painting – Hooker's Green, Payne's Grey, Burnt Sienna, Titanium White, Lemon Yellow and Raw Umber – and chose Daler Line and Wash Board as a support. The sky and foreground were suggested with loose washes which were a mixture of Hooker's Green plus a little Lemon Yellow added to Titanium White and applied with a 25 mm (1 in) wash brush. I used Burnt Sienna and Raw Umber for the warm washes on the buildings.

Second stage (fig. 39) A layer of thin acrylic paint on a Line and Wash Board makes a pleasant surface to draw on, and I kept my charcoal pencil well sharpened for the initial crisp line work. I placed the tallest chimney on the central building first and then judged distances between the other chimney stacks and so on. No attempt was made to superimpose the drawing exactly in line with the washes, which can be adjusted once the drawing is complete and more colour added. Payne's Grey was introduced on roofs and in shadow areas.

Fig. 38 **First stage**

Fig. 39 **Second stage**

Fig. 40   Finished stage, *Smethwick Canal*, charcoal and acrylic, 30.5 × 40.5 cm (12 × 16 in)

Finished stage (fig. 40)   So far all the acrylic paint has been diluted with water and applied as transparent colour washes. Now I started to build up a thickness of paint to create textures and capture a feeling of soft wintery light, but first I adjusted the sky with a semi-dilute wash of pale green grey. This subtle colour was repeated on the foreground, thus linking it to the sky and giving some unity to the painting, just as a limited palette will give unity.

When I first started this painting I had already decided where the lightest areas would be. I wanted to focus the light on the building behind the lamp-post as a balance to the wider dark shape of the bridge. You may have noticed at the second stage of the painting that the wash on this building was quite dark in tone.

This was deliberately done as an undercolour that could be allowed to break through a subsequent layer of thick paint. I mixed Titanium White with a little Lemon Yellow without any water, and applied it with a palette knife, the idea being to represent crumbling stucco with darker brick beneath. This creamy lemon colour was also introduced on other light areas in the painting, mostly applied with the palette knife except for the chimneys which needed the more precise touch of a small brush.

Having established the lightest areas, I gradually worked thicker paint over the middle tones, strengthening the colour in places. Sometimes this paint broke into the charcoal pencil, giving an interesting graphic quality to the line work. Most of the original thin washes have been retained in the dark areas of the painting, some darkened further with a layer of soft charcoal shading. I wanted to portray an impression of industrial smut clinging to part of the brickwork, and the introduction of soft charcoal stick dragged over the paint seemed to work well. Here and there I rubbed the charcoal with my finger and on other areas I drew details with the end of the stick.

At this point the colours were very subtle and subdued by the addition of charcoal, and I thought the painting needed a little surprise element, so I added a small area of strong green on the warehouse door. Finally a few details were added with charcoal pencil and then I sprayed a little fixative over the whole painting.

The detail in **fig. 41** shows the versatility of the acrylic medium and the contrast in surface quality between thick and thin paint. The roof of the building is painted with transparent washes of Burnt Sienna, Hooker's Green and a little Raw Umber in just the same manner as a watercolour, whereas the creamy face of the building is painted with thick impasto applied with a palette knife so that it actually stands up from the Daler board, just as in an oil painting. Touches of the first thin washes show through the impasto.

The detail in **fig. 42** shows the crumbling texture of the old brick bridge, which has been achieved by allowing the first washes to show through subsequent subtle washes and then dragging a layer of soft charcoal on top. A hint of detail drawn with charcoal pencil added substance to the bridge.

Fig. 41   Detail of fig. 40

Fig. 42   Detail of fig. 40

WATERCOLOUR AND GOUACHE

Fig. 43

Fig. 44 *Coast*, exercise in watercolour and gouache

Fig. 45 *Blue Trees*, exercise in watercolour and gouache

Transparent watercolour and opaque gouache co-exist particularly well because they are both water-based media and therefore technically compatible. They also coexist successfully on a visual level where the contrast between thin and thick paint is very pleasing to the eye. It is characteristic of gouache paint that you can work from dark to light, and paint on a variety of supports with any type of brush.

Coast I started with transparent watercolour washes, which were allowed to dry before I superimposed washes of dilute gouache and finally added some areas of thickly applied paint. It is wise to have a separate palette or saucer for gouache paint so that it does not interfere with the transparency of the paint in your watercolour box.

In **fig. 43** I used a small piece of Bockingford NOT 300 gsm (140 lb) watercolour paper measuring 13×20.5 cm (5×8 in) and gave it an all-over wash of Raw Sienna watercolour with a No. 7 sable brush. I outlined the foreground with Olive Green and Burnt Umber which I also used to paint the nearest field and central cliff. The distant cliff is cooler in colour and for this I used Cobalt Blue greyed with a little Burnt Umber which I also washed over the foreground.

When the washes were dry (**fig. 44**), I brushed dilute Cool Grey 1 gouache over the cliffs, leaving touches of the underwash showing through. The green fields and sandy bay were painted with thicker gouache using various mixtures of Lemon Yellow, Olive Green and Raw Sienna added to Permanent White. Finally I added Cool Grey light on the water.

Blue Trees (fig. 45) The blue trees are also painted on watercolour paper, and to achieve a wintery atmosphere I washed pale French Ultramarine watercolour all over the paper. Before this had completely dried, I brushed in some Burnt Umber to suggest branches and distant trees. These two pigments tend to precipitate when painted wet-in-wet and I retained some of the granular effects in the painting. Tree trunks were painted with a darker mixture of French Ultramarine and Burnt Umber and then the painting was left to dry.

Fig. 46

Fig. 47 *The Barn*, **exercise in watercolour and gouache**

I changed to my gouache palette and mixed a subtle creamy colour for the clouds with Neutral Grey 1 and Permanent White, suggesting glimpses of sky through the trees by overpainting areas of the original watercolour wash and leaving parts to create more branches. Finally I used a little Yellow Ochre and Permanent White gouache to create a touch of warmer light on some of the branches and trunks on the left.

The Barn is an exercise that uses watercolour and gouache on a toned grey paper, allowing some of the paper to show in the painting. In **fig. 46** I have used Burnt Umber and Olive Green transparent watercolour as a monochrome, carefully chosen so that it could be left to show as the dark areas, and be in keeping with the weathered stonework.

All the colour work is painted with gouache in **fig. 47**, quite thickly to cover the sky and with a dry brush across the farmyard, allowing some grey paper to show. Dilute gouache at the top of the barn wall allows the monochrome to show through and some stones have been picked out in more detail with a thicker covering of paint.

Gateway (fig. 48) The tree by the gate is another exercise on grey paper, begun in the same way as the barn with transparent watercolour washes overlaid with opaque gouache paint.

Fig. 48 *Gateway*, **exercise in watercolour and gouache**

Demonstration 3: Still Life with Geraniums

In this painting I have combined watercolour and gouache again, this time on Saunders Waterford NOT 300 gsm (140 lb) watercolour paper. The first watercolour washes are bright basic colours (**fig. 49**) which I intend to soften with subsequent layers of semi-opaque gouache paint. I usually commence painting without any preliminary drawing, preferring the freedom of the blank paper, but I am fully aware that not everyone is confident to work in this way. So, for this demonstration of a rather complicated subject, I have drawn a very minimal pencil outline without any shading.

First stage (**fig. 50**)   The first wash is of Cadmium Yellow applied with a large wash brush. I did not worry about keeping precisely to the pencil lines, and left parts of the flowers as white paper. Next I prepared a large quantity of Hooker's Green 1 wash in a saucer and used the large brush again to paint the

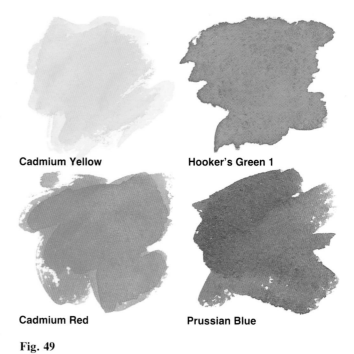

Cadmium Yellow   Hooker's Green 1

Cadmium Red   Prussian Blue

Fig. 49

Fig. 50   First stage

32

Fig. 51 Second stage

background, quickly working round the edges of flowers and fruit with the tip of the brush before the wash was dry.

Second stage (fig. 51) Here you can see the green background wash completed and a paler green wash taken over the leaves. I changed to a No. 7 sable to paint the flowers, using Cadmium Red and touches of Crimson Alizarin. There are lovely variations of orange where the red colour has flooded over the first yellow washes. When the flowers were dry, I darkened the background with Prussian Blue, again preparing a large amount of wash.

The detail (**fig. 52**) shows how freely the Cadmium Red has been brushed over the flower heads, simply registering them as an area of colour, whereas the dark colour on the background has been painted with a little more precision. Notice that the stem, which is part of the first pale green wash, only became defined once I had painted the dark background on each side.

Fig. 52 Detail of fig. 51

Fig. 53 Third stage

Third stage (fig. 53) The Prussian Blue wash has also been used to define the flower pot and to suggest cool shadows on and under the leaves. I added Burnt Umber to the blue wash to make a very strong dark tone for part of the background and between the leaves.

The painting was now developed with gouache paint, starting with the flowers. Some of their bright colours have been softened by overpainting with dilute Permanent White and some petals were painted with touches of Cadmium Red (Hue), Middle Orange or Brilliant Yellow added to the white. On other petals the original transparent watercolour wash was left untouched. Next I added a little Ultramarine to the remainder of the pink and orange flower mix and painted this thinly over the mugs. This lowered their tone and helped to create some unity within the painting.

Finished stage (fig. 54) A gradual harmonizing of colours and adjustment of tones continued over the painting as a whole by the addition of thin layers of gouache. Taking up the large brush again, I softened

the background by painting a film of dilute blue grey colour over it – a mixture of Ultramarine and Neutral Grey 1. Then I added some Permanent White to the mix to develop the foreground, thickening the paint on light areas and leaving the original dark transparent watercolour to give depth to the shadows. The first washes of Hooker's Green watercolour still permeate the painting but the leaves and apples are now the dominant green, although the apples have been considerably lowered in tone with gouache.

Next the flower heads were more fully worked out and the shape of the petals refined by drawing with a very thin No. 000 sable brush and Cadmium Red. The detail in **fig. 55** shows the working out more clearly, and it is interesting to refer back to the detail from the second stage (page 33) and realize how much the painting has developed since the first watercolour washes were made.

Fig. 56 shows more of the fine brushwork which it is possible to superimpose with the covering power of gouache paint. Finally I worked on the leaves, refining their shapes and suggesting some of the veins with the No. 000 brush and dark green paint.

34

Fig. 54 Finished stage, *Still Life with Geraniums*, watercolour and gouache, 43 × 56.5 cm (17 × 22¼ in)

Fig. 55 Detail of fig. 54

Fig. 56 Detail of fig. 54

Watercolour, gouache and pastel pencils

In these paintings I have added pastel pencils to watercolour and gouache. It is interesting to combine painting and graphic techniques in one image, and the soft texture of pastel pencil unites well with the smooth surface of these water-based media.

Still Life with Pots and Spotted Cloth   The still life (**fig. 57**) was painted with loose transparent washes and the objects drawn with coloured pastel pencils in Sanguine and Olive Green. Light tones and patterns were then established with gouache paint, sometimes diluted, and finally textures were added with pastel pencils.

In most transparent watercolour painting processes the lightest tones are created first, the darkest tones being gradually developed at the end. But here, the introduction of gouache paint, which is an opaque watercolour medium, has enabled me to use its covering power to superimpose highlights on a dark wash wherever I want them.

Saundersfoot Harbour   It was a cold dull day when I sat on the quayside to make this harbour painting (**fig. 58**), but in spite of the uninspiring weather I was excited by the variety and pattern of boat shapes which really caught my eye.

I worked on mid-grey pastel paper, this time starting with a dark grey pastel pencil drawing. To this I added soft washes of transparent watercolour, using a mixture of Burnt Sienna and Prussian Blue. A 38 mm (1½ in) house painter's brush is wonderful for these preliminary washes and enables me to work loosely and at speed. In the background I allowed Prussian Blue to dominate the wash mixture to give a feeling of recession, but in the foreground Burnt Sienna was more dominant except for the shadow areas beneath the boats. Although these colours are both powerful, they become muted as they sink into the grey paper. I changed to a relatively smaller brush and deepened the washes over darker areas. For the strongest darks I added some Burnt Umber or French Ultramarine to the wash.

Over the sky I used a very pale dilute wash of Permanent White and Ultramarine gouache and this allowed a hint of grey paper to show through, keeping the colour subtle. Other light tones in the painting are mixtures of white with Raw Umber or Raw Sienna, Cool Grey 1 with Raw Sienna, and a few touches of pure white. I used a fine brush to touch in the seagulls and finally reverted to pastel pencils to add details.

Fig. 57   *Still Life with Pots and Spotted Cloth*, watercolour, gouache and pastel pencils, 35.5 × 43 cm (14 × 17 in)

36

Fig. 58 *Saundersfoot Harbour*, watercolour, gouache and pastel pencils, 48 × 32 cm (19 × 12½ in)

DRAWING WITH MIXED MEDIA

We have all tried to express our ideas and put down what we see by means of a line drawing and this is an essential part of learning to know a subject. It is also very rewarding to expand our range of drawing media and perhaps find an interesting, more personal means of expression. Recently I was looking at reproductions of drawings by Leonardo da Vinci and he worked with black, white and red chalks on colourful grounds, some red, some orange, pink or green. He also used a combination of pen and ink, brown wash and black chalk on a single drawing. Other artists in the sixteenth century, such as Tintoretto and Dürer, made drawings on coloured grounds with pencil or sanguine chalk and white paint.

Winter Landscape This little snowscape sketch in **fig. 59** was drawn with black charcoal pencil over gouache paint on blue pastel paper. I chose blue to heighten the effect of the snow scene, allowing the

paper to portray the cool shadows and distant hill. The sketch started with a simple line drawing followed by dilute washes of Permanent White gouache paint, gradually increasing the thickness of paint on the lightest areas. More dark pencil work was superimposed to complete the sketch. This is quite a speedy way of gathering information on a cold day.

Shena My sketch of Shena (**fig. 60**) was made on gold coloured Ingres paper with a black Conté drawing pencil and white gouache. A black line drawing always looks very effective on a coloured ground, and to make the drawing more tonal, I flooded the light areas with white gouache. The paper then worked as the middle tones.

Try drawing still-life groups or plants as Leonardo did, with black, white and sanguine chalk or today's equivalent, the hard square-ended variety of pastel crayon, on different coloured pastel papers.

Fig. 59 *Winter Landscape,* **gouache and charcoal pencil, 16.5 × 29 cm (6½ × 11½ in)**

Fig. 60 *Shena*, gouache and Conté drawing pencil, 37 × 28.5 cm (14½ × 11¼ in)

Fig. 61　*Samantha*, watercolour, gouache and black pencil,　33.5 × 28 cm (13¼ × 11 in)

Drawing figure studies

These figure studies are very subtle in colour. Combining delicate watercolour washes and pencil on white paper, they can truly be called watercolour drawings. This is a traditional way of working practised through the centuries. The drawing of Samantha (**fig. 61**) has been heightened with white gouache, and the self-portrait (**fig. 62**) was made with Sanguine and Grey Conté pencils and watercolour.

When you are drawing figures or portraits it is preferable, if at all possible, to use an easel – so that you can stand back from your work and view both the model and your drawing. In this way it is easier to see how the proportions are progressing. Working at an easel also enables you to distance yourself from the paper, so that you can use your whole arm and draw more freely. I often lightly draw faint lines to establish the relative positions of features. It is important to look for the tilt of the head, the level of the ears in comparison with the nose, and the shape of the hair. Drawing demands continual measuring up with the eye, looking for reference points and comparing one measurement with another.

Samantha　The drawing of Samantha was made on watercolour paper with a black drawing pencil and you can see that the texture of the paper has created a

40

Fig. 62 *Self-Portrait*, watercolour and Conté pastel pencils, 42 × 44 cm (16½ × 17¼ in)

soft broken line, particularly noticeable on the hair. I applied only a slight amount of pencil shading to the face; the main shadows were modelled with a brush and Brown Madder watercolour.

A hazard of working in watercolour at an easel is that the washes tend to run down the vertical paper surface. Here I diverted some of the inadvertent runs to follow the line of the shoulders, and added a wash of French Ultramarine over the jumper to blend in with the other runs.

Self-Portrait If you are unable to find a model, try drawing yourself. Most artists have used themselves as models at some time or other. This quick sketch of

myself in the studio came about unexpectedly. I have been working in this studio for years, and then, one morning, I caught sight of myself in the big studio mirror and was instantly attracted to the view of the old wooden door and the Degas poster behind me. As I started to draw, I began to see the studio with fresh eyes as a pattern of squares and rectangles echoing the shapes of the door and poster. The colours that I saw reflected in the mirror were in sympathy with my leather jerkin and grey checked shirt, and there seemed to be a visual unity about the whole image.

WATERCOLOUR AND PASTEL

Fig. 63 *Wellington Street, London WC2*, **watercolour and pastel, 65 × 49.5 cm (25½ × 19½ in)**

Here I am introducing two media which work very well together in a similar way to watercolour and gouache, where there is interplay between a thin transparent medium and a thicker opaque medium. Pastel, like gouache, is most effective when applied to a toned or coloured ground where its opaque qualities are most obvious.

This combination of mixed media can be painted on watercolour, cartridge or pastel paper, or Ingres mounting board. A support with some texture is best, so that the pastel can adhere to the surface, and watercolour is an ideal partner because it sinks into the support without filling the grain. Pastel can be applied successfully over watercolour by drawing with the tip, rubbing and blending with fingers or a torchon, or by painting with the side of the pastel. Fine details can be introduced with pastel pencils which are harder than soft pastels.

Wellington Street, London (fig. 63) This is a completed painting based on a quick pen sketch of a London street and was painted on blue pastel paper. The colour of the paper has had a strong effect on this painting. I started with broad warm washes of Burnt Sienna and Burnt Umber and then overpainted with pastel. I liked the varied solid shapes of the buildings, which prompted me to paint them with large slabs of colour. Notice that I have introduced blue into the buildings echoing the colour of the sky. I was also attracted by the hoardings which contributed design and pattern to the street scene.

Robin Hood's Bay 1 and 2 The colour beginnings in **figs. 64** and **65** show watercolour used as a tonal underpainting on the blue paper and as a brightly

Fig. 64 *Robin Hood's Bay 1*, **watercolour and pastel, 66 × 43 cm (26 × 17 in)**

Fig. 65 *Robin Hood's Bay 2*, watercolour and pastel, 49 × 56.5 cm (19¼ × 22¼ in)

coloured basis on the light buff paper. Both paintings were inspired by sketches I made at Robin Hood's Bay on the Yorkshire coast and are unfinished to show work in progress.

The first painting (**fig. 64**), on blue pastel paper, was started in the studio and is based on a black-and-white sketch. You might have expected me to start the large-scale work by drawing an outline of the buildings, but here I started by massing in the dark areas of the project using flat brushes. The roofs were painted in one broad band of watercolour with a 38 mm (1½ in) house painter's brush, using a mixture of Burnt Umber and Payne's Grey. All the under-painting was restricted to these two colours, and I varied the tones on the dark parts of the buildings and strengthened the washes on the windows. At this stage the brush work was very broad and unfussy, simply establishing the main elements in the painting. Then I started to add pastel, beginning with the sky and defining chimneys and roof-tops a little more precisely. Some warm-coloured pastel was dragged over

the walls with light pressure which allowed the colour of the paper to show through. The choice of coloured ground is important since it plays a part and influences the finished painting.

The second painting of Robin Hood's Bay (**fig. 65**), on light buff-coloured pastel paper, is unfinished because it was started on site and I aimed to record enough essential structure, layout, colour and detail to enable me to finish the painting in the studio. By doing this I can make the most of my time on site, and then study the work in the studio with a fresh eye as to how I wish to interpret the subject.

I started with bright watercolour washes of Sap Green and Burnt Sienna, darkening the sky with Lamp Black. Line work and details were put in with a sable brush and Lamp Black at full strength. In this way I created a choice of colour and tone as a basis for superimposing warm or cool pastel. Pale Blue Grey and Purple Grey pastel have been worked over the dark sky, allowing some of the wash to show as an interesting texture.

43

Fig. 66

Demonstration 4: Alstonefield

This cluster of cottages is in the Derbyshire Peak District where I sometimes paint. The sketch (**fig. 66**) was made with a fibre-tip pen and in it I have observed the contrasting areas of light on the buildings against the dark tones of the roofs and foliage. For the painting I chose green heavy-weight pastel paper, its colour being appropriate to the landscape.

First stage (**fig. 67**)   I blocked in the mass of the buildings using a large brush, indicating dark areas with a mixture of Hooker's Green and Burnt Umber watercolour. Windows and chimneys were drawn in simply with Burnt Umber, using a smaller brush, and the fields were painted with Hooker's Green. This stage establishes the pattern of lights and darks.

Second stage (**fig. 68**)   When the watercolour washes were dry, I added Warm Grey Tint 3, Cool Grey Tint 2 and Purple Grey Tint 0 pastel to the cottage walls and a little to the roofs to suggest tiles. Some of the pastel was lightly scumbled over the walls so that the cool green showed through. I also introduced a hint of warm colour on one of the buildings with Burnt Umber Tint 1.

Finished stage (**fig. 69**)   I realized that the foreground and distant fields were too light and dominant, so I added a wash of dilute Burnt Umber to lower the tone. Then I refined the overall drawing with brown and white pastel pencils for details, and finally added Grass Green Tint 4 between the tree branches and across the distant field.

Fig. 67   **First stage**

Fig. 68   **Second stage**

44

Fig. 69   Finished stage, *Alstonefield*, watercolour and pastel, 32 × 25 cm (12½ × 9¾ in)

PRINTING INK AND OTHER MEDIA

Fig. 70

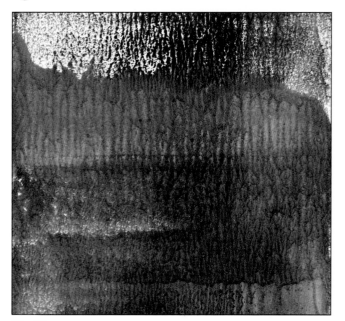

Fig. 71

As you have already seen, pastel marries well with watercolour. It can also be successfully combined with oil-based media and, in this section, I have added pastel to images made with black printing ink. Later I include watercolour and gouache too, but first I will describe how I prepared these preliminary papers.

In **fig. 70** I have used brown Ingres pastel paper and the texture can be clearly seen. I squeezed Daler Rowney oil-based Black Block Printing Colour onto a glass slab (or smooth plastic would do) and spread it out fairly evenly with a roller. The ink was then rolled onto the paper, making a very dark impression whilst the roller was fully inked, but becoming fainter as the ink was dispersed. Narrow marks were achieved by pressing the roller onto the paper and lifting it off again without any rolling action.

The roller marks in **fig. 71** were made on a smooth-surfaced card with printing ink diluted with turpentine. I often prepare these papers at the end of a printing session when I am cleaning up the glass and roller. In doing so, I pour turpentine onto the inky roller, and I then roll it out onto different supports. The effects vary according to the amount of turpentine and the type of support. These unpredictable impressions can often suggest a subject, and be the starting point for a painting.

In **fig. 72** I have rolled ink onto the smooth side of a heavy-weight red pastel paper, in horizontal and vertical directions which overlap in the centre giving dark passages. Lighter-toned textures have been created by continuing to roll out in random directions as the ink dries off. This allows more of the red paper to show through. Thin broken lines were achieved by the briefest of contacts of roller onto paper with a staccato action. Finally, I rolled some areas with dilute ink. This image brings to my mind an industrial landscape, but the viewer might have other ideas.

Still Life by the Window   Once again textured Ingres paper is the support for these roller images (**fig. 73**) which form the basis for my still-life painting. I usually leave these prepared papers to dry out for a day before adding other media.

Printing ink dries with a fairly matt surface, especially where turpentine has been added, and this quality harmonizes well with pastel. I drew the still life (**fig. 74**) with square-ended pastels and then worked with softer pastel, blending it over some of the ink and allowing other areas of ink or paper to show through.

46

Fig. 72

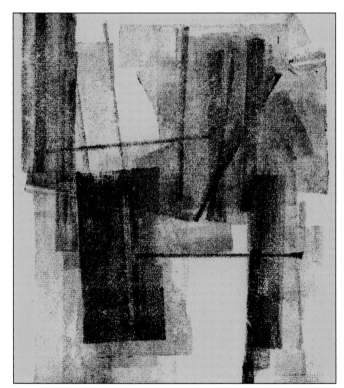

Fig. 73

Fig. 74 *Still Life by the Window*, printing ink and pastel, 25.5 × 21.5 cm (10 × 8½ in)

Fig. 75

Monotype with watercolour and pastel

On pages 46 and 47 I made roller images with printing ink. Here I am using an inked glass slab to create a monotype. This is a very simple method of printing but, as the name implies, you only make one print at a time. Castiglione is reputed to have invented the monotype in the seventeenth century and Degas also practised this technique.

Oil paint or printing ink is painted onto a metal plate or glass, a piece of paper is laid onto it, and an impression is taken by rubbing over the back of the paper by hand or by passing it through a press. The pressure of the printing will transfer the paint or ink onto the paper to produce an interesting textured reverse image. Sometimes a second impression can be taken before the paint or ink dries, but the image will be less distinct.

Snowdonia 1   After a recent visit to North Wales, mountains were on my mind, and one of my sketches became the basis for this monotype (**fig. 75**). First of all I squeezed out some Rowney Black Block Printing Colour onto a glass slab and rolled it out evenly. Then I scratched the outlines of the mountain and lake onto the inked surface, using a palette knife (or you could use the handle of an old brush). Taking up a turpsy rag, I proceeded to wipe off the printing ink over the areas of sky and water.

To print the monotype, I placed a piece of cartridge paper over the inked glass and rubbed over the back of the paper with the palm of my hand (or you could use a rag). Before peeling the paper off completely, I usually lift one corner to see if the impression is satisfactory, and, if necessary, I rub it again using more pressure. The texture and weight of paper used for printing will influence the texture and graphic quality

Fig. 76   *Snowdonia 1*, monotype with watercolour and pastel, 18 × 26 cm (7 × 10¼ in)

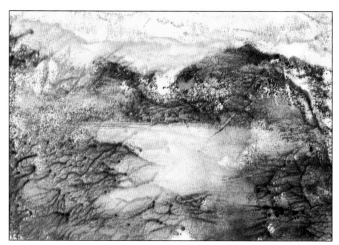

Fig. 77

pencil while the paper was still damp, resulting in a soft diffused line. More colour and details were added with Green Grey Tint 4, Cool Grey Tint 5 and Raw Sienna Tint 1 soft pastels and green pastel pencil, but much of the original printing ink remains.

Snowdonia 2 I re-inked the glass with the roller and repeated the process of scratching the outlines of the mountain and lake and wiping away light areas with a rag. Different effects were created on this image (**fig. 77**) by rubbing over the back of the paper with a turpsy rag. The turpentine sinks through the paper, making it transparent and enabling you to see the ink thinning and spreading on the glass. The image began to dissolve in different directions, and I lifted the paper off the glass quickly.

The results of this technique are interesting but unpredictable, and sometimes very rewarding. I spread all my experimental monotypes out to dry for a day or two before working over them with other media.

The haphazard effects on this basic image led to a different interpretation of the subject (**fig. 78**). Some of the runs looked like wind-blown trees and wild undergrowth around the lake. Once again, I have worked watercolour and pastel pencils over the original monotype.

of the print. Mine was a heavy cartridge paper with a slight texture and the ink was beginning to dry under the studio lights, so the print has a grainy quality which made a good texture for the mountains.

After leaving the monotype to dry for a day, I added watercolour washes (**fig. 76**), first an overall wash of pale Cadmium Red and then a wash of Prussian Blue with a touch of Lamp Black, introducing a hint of Raw Sienna in the foreground. I defined the mountain profiles by drawing with a grey pastel

Fig. 78 *Snowdonia 2*, **monotype with watercolour and pastel, 18 × 26 cm (7 × 10¼ in)**

Monotype with watercolour and gouache

These monotypes are totally abstract images, made by dropping turpentine onto inked glass and either tilting the glass so that the turpentine runs in random directions, or manipulating the turpentine with a trowel-shaped palette knife. Then an impression is taken. I might make several impressions before choosing those that are most visually exciting.

When I looked at **fig. 79** vertically I imagined a figure, but horizontally I could see a windy sea-shore with boats and seaweed. In **fig. 80** I added water-colour and a small amount of drawing with pastel pencil. Gouache was introduced onto clouds and the lighthouse, and a few over-inked areas adjusted with this opaque paint.

I was so excited by the abstract print shown in **fig. 81** that I have included it on its own. Again, I can visualize standing figures, but looked at horizontally the ink blobs become trees and the scraped lines could be ploughed fields.

Fig. 79

Fig. 80 *Sea-shore*, monotype with watercolour and gouache, 18 × 23 cm (7 × 9 in)

Fig. 81   *Abstract*, monotype, 25.5 × 21 cm (10 × 8¼ in)

OIL PAINT AND PASTEL

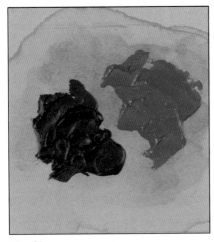

Fig. 82

Fig. 83a

Fig. 83b

This is the combination of media which surprises people the most, but it is not a new idea. In the seventeenth century, Castiglione (who invented the monotype) was making chalk drawings over thin washes of oil paint. In the latter half of the nineteenth century Degas, Mary Cassatt and Toulouse Lautrec were some of the artists painting in oil and pastel and also pastel over monotype.

Stiff paper or board can be used and I prepare grounds in advance so that they are dry for the pastel work. **Fig. 82** shows how I squeeze oil paint onto blotting paper and leave it overnight to absorb some of the oil.

Next day I mix the oil paint with distilled turpentine and brush it over the support with a hog brush (**fig. 83a**), avoiding thick blobs of paint by using a good-quality oil paint that will dissolve easily in a wash.

When the paint is dry I can work on top with soft pastel (**fig. 83b**). Here I have blended some of the pastel into the oil ground with a hog brush.

Estuary (fig. 84)   When oil paint is thinned down with distilled turpentine, it becomes fluid and partially transparent. Here I am using Daler Line and Wash Board and these soft overlapping washes of Cobalt Blue and Raw Umber have sunk into the surface with a pleasing, slightly mottled texture. I have begun to add soft pastel, using the palest tints of Coeruleum, Yellow Ochre and French Ultramarine, sometimes blending it into the oil ground with my fingers. I aim to keep a soft misty effect.

Landscape with Red Hill (fig. 85)   This is another beginning showing the process of working over and incorporating the oil ground. I used Whatman 300 gsm (140 lb) Hot Pressed watercolour paper and brushed it over with dilute Viridian and Mars Red oil paint. I then gently laid a piece of paper on top of the wet paint and almost immediately lifted if off, creating irregular areas of mottled paint. Darker tones were brushed on with Mars Red and a little Lamp Black to break across the mottled texture. Next day I drew the landscape with dark Purple Brown pastel and started to introduce soft greens onto the fields.

Fig. 84 (opposite above)   *Estuary*, oil paint and pastel, 23 × 44 cm (9 × 17¼ in)

Fig. 85 (opposite)   *Landscape with Red Hill*, oil paint and pastel, 25.5 × 36 cm (10 × 14¼ in)

Fig. 86

Fig. 87 *Aquilegia*, oil paint and pastel, 16 × 13.5 cm
(6¼ × 5¼ in)

Flowers in oil paint and pastel

I thought the warm pinks and mauves of these flower pieces could be shown to advantage against a green background. The green ground behind the small study of the aquilegia plant is subtle, a mixture of Raw Umber and Viridian oil paint, whereas the brightly coloured sweet williams can take a stronger green background. Here I used an underpainting built up of layers of Viridian, Cadmium Yellow and Lamp Black.

These prepared grounds are painted on heavy cartridge paper with a large hog bristle brush and oil paint previously dried out on blotting paper, then diluted with a little distilled turpentine as already explained on page 52. On smooth paper such as this, the paint can be pushed around with the brush or a palette knife and the strokes are more obvious. The paint dries out with a matt velvety surface which feels good to work on with soft pastel.

Aquilegia A pale green square-ended pastel was used to outline the plant against the dark-toned ground (**fig. 86**). Square pastels are usually of a hard enough quality to make it possible to draw fine lines. At this stage I decided that most of the random brush marks on the background could be retained to represent general foliage.

All the painting from now on was with soft pastel (**fig. 87**). Light and shade was suggested on each flower, allowing the background to show through a thin layer of pastel in shaded areas and pressing the pastel on more solidly to emphasize the light areas. I also achieved light and shade on a petal by applying pastel firmly all over and then brushing some of it into the background where I wanted a soft shadow. You can also blend the pastel into the background with your fingers.

Pinks and Sweet Williams (fig. 88) The brushstrokes on this background flow in vertical and horizontal directions which created a suitable setting for this group, the vertical brushstrokes representing a hanging backcloth, and the horizontal brush strokes describing a flat surface. The densely packed flowerheads of the sweet william plant provided a variety of pink, peach, mauve and deep red colours and I liked their mass in contrast to the slim flowerheads of the pinks.

The detail in **fig. 89** shows the fringed petals of the pinks painted in pastel over the striped brush marks of the oil-based backcloth.

Fig. 88   *Pinks and Sweet Williams*, oil paint and pastel, 28 × 33.5 cm (11 × 13¼ in)

Fig. 89   Detail of fig. 88

INDIAN INK AND OIL PASTEL

Fig. 90

Fig. 91

Using oil pastel

I have already discussed various ways of using soft pastels earlier in the book. Now we will look at oil pastels, which have a very different composition and application. Whereas soft pastels are dry pigment mixed with a binder, these are pigments mixed with wax and oil; they produce an entirely different paint surface and have their own unique painting possibilities. For example, oil pastels can be used in successive layers of different colours. You can then scratch through the final layer with a sharp blade so that the underlying colour is revealed, or through even further to reveal the first of the layers.

Oil pastel can be applied directly like a crayon to make lines or as a solid area of colour. The end of the pastel stick can be dipped in turpentine to give a softer blurred line, or an area of pastel can be brushed over with turpentine to create washes of colour. Colours can also be blended with fingers or a turpsy rag.

Oil pastels are of a soft consistency and can be very sticky in hot weather, so it is wise to hold them by their paper wrappers. By their nature they are not a medium for fine details, but require a broad, free treatment.

Supports for oil pastel

Oil pastel paintings can be made on a variety of surfaces, but it is best to work on a rigid support such as a heavy 300 gsm (140 lb) watercolour paper (either NOT or Hot Pressed), oil-painting paper or board. You can also paint on primed hardboard. Canvas is too floppy and dents easily under the pressure of the painting stick.

Oil pastel with other media

Oil pastel can be used in conjunction with other media. It is useful for preliminary mapping-in on an oil painting or, at a later stage, for making additions to an oil painting. The pastel also works well over washes of watercolour, acrylic, gouache or ink.

With watercolours it can be used as a resist: lines of pastel are drawn first and then washed over with watercolour to achieve interesting effects. Sometimes, I brush black Indian ink over the paper, and when it is dry I work pastel on top, leaving some areas uncovered or scratching and scraping through to reveal the ink.

Because these pastels are oil-based they take time to dry out; this will vary between one to five days depending on the manufacturer and the thickness of their application.

Fig. 90 shows scribbles of oil pastel freely applied, while in **fig. 91** the same scribbles are blended with a hog bristle brush and turpentine. In **fig. 92**, oil pastel is worked over dry Indian ink. Where the colour is applied with medium pressure, the ink shows through enough to lower the tone. Where heavily applied, the pastel has good covering power. Oil pastel is again worked over Indian ink in **fig. 93**, then scratched through with a sharp blade to reveal the ink.

In **fig. 94**, Indian ink is flooded over oil pastel. Some is repelled and oil pastel shows through. **Fig. 95** shows dilute Indian ink over oil pastel. Here some adheres to the pastel and lowers the tone.

Fig. 92

Fig. 93

Fig. 94

Fig. 95

Fig. 96

Demonstration 5: Polperro

This demonstration was based on a sketch (**fig. 96**) I made in Cornwall some time ago, and I have employed some of the techniques already shown on pages 56 and 57.

First stage (fig. 97) I used Blue Grey Ingres mounting board, and brushed in the cottages with soft grey tones of dilute Indian ink. Then I drew the outlines with a No. 7 sable brush and undiluted ink.

Second stage (fig. 98) I completed the drawing, keeping it very simple, and filled in the darks as flat areas without modelling or much detail. I strengthened some of the grey areas with further washes of dilute ink and let them dry before starting with oil pastel. Then I began to paint the sky using strokes of dark Prussian Blue, Ultramarine Blue and White.

Finished stage (fig. 99) I continued to add oil pastel to the sky and then brushed it over with turpentine to blend the colours into one flat area of blue, repeating this colour on the foreground shed. Most of the light areas were painted with layers of pale Orange, Lemon Yellow and White oil pastel, and the mid tones with random strokes of Light Grey and a little Pink, allowing some ink washes to show through.

Fig. 97 First stage

Fig. 98 Second stage

Fig. 99   Finished stage, *Polperro*, Indian ink and oil pastel,   32 × 24 cm (12½ × 9½ in)

The black wall was painted all over with a mixture of Dark Grey and Prussian Blue oil pastel, and then scratched through to indicate the wall-hung slates. Similarly, black windows were covered in Light Grey pastel and the panes scraped away to reveal black ink, leaving narrow grey window bars between. I indicated some foliage in the pots and grass in the foreground with Olive Green oil pastel and painted the doors with deep Prussian Blue. A few touches of Burnt Sienna and a warm brown provided a foil to the cool blues.

59

OIL PASTEL AND ACRYLIC

Fig. 100

Fig. 101

Earlier in the book, on pages 26–29, I used acrylic paint with charcoal; now I am pairing acrylic with oil pastel. Acrylic adheres to any grease-free surface and it dries quickly with a matt finish which makes a good surface to take an oil-based medium. Water is used to thin the paint and make transparent washes, but it is an opaque medium when used straight from the tube. There are also various acrylic media which can be mixed with the paint to retard drying time, add gloss, make glazes or build up impasto.

Acrylic is a permanent medium and, once dry, cannot be washed off, which means that the first washes laid will not be disturbed by any subsequent work. Because of its fast-drying nature it is imperative to replace caps immediately, keep brushes moist, and make sure that they are thoroughly washed when painting is over.

Oil pastel can be worked successfully on top of thin or thick acrylic paint and these doodles show a few of the techniques.

Fig. 100 shows a thin Ultramarine acrylic wash with Orange oil pastel worked on top. In **fig. 101** a thin blue wash has impasto medium superimposed with a palette knife. I use Rowney Texture Paste as a medium. Note that the drying time of Texture Paste varies between 10 minutes to one hour depending on the thickness.

In **fig. 102** the Texture Paste was tinted with Ultramarine and applied with a palette knife. When dry, a dilute wash of Rowney Orange acrylic was brushed over, gathering between the ridges of impasto. Thick blue-tinted impasto was applied in **fig. 103** and, when dry, Orange oil pastel was crayoned across the surface. It adheres to the raised ridges in the Texture Paste.

For **fig. 104** Rowney Orange and Monestial Blue acrylic were mixed together to give a dark green. Three broad bands of zigzag pattern were painted with orange and gold oil pastel and superimposed on the green. The oil pastel was scratched through with a sharp blade to reveal the dark green background.

Orange oil pastel was applied to the support in **fig. 105** and then brushed over with a semi-transparent dark green acrylic wash. The wash was scratched through with a sharp blade to reveal the Orange oil pastel beneath.

60

Fig. 102

Fig. 103

Fig. 104

Fig. 105

Fig. 106   First stage

Demonstration 6: Arabic *Dellahs*

This demonstration is based on some drawings I made of Arabic *dellahs* in the Sadu House museum in Kuwait city. They are exciting shapes and each one has its own individual design. I aim to use some of the techniques already described on pages 60 and 61 and create a variety of surface textures within the painting with thin washes of acrylic, thick impasto using Texture Paste, and oil pastel, including Gold.

First stage (fig. 106)   I started the painting with a cool blue monochrome as a contrast to the Gold pastel and warmth of the other colours. The support is a thick piece of smooth watercolour paper sturdy enough to take the ensuing layers of impasto, and I used a 'Stay-Wet' palette to keep my paint moist for a long time. Ultramarine acrylic paint was diluted with water and the subject drawn with a No. 5 sable brush. I used a larger sable for the blue background washes. Then the shapes of the *dellahs* were given more definition by outlining with less dilute paint.

Second stage (fig. 107)   I mixed Monestial Blue with acrylic Texture Paste to form a thick impasto for the crumbling wall texture behind the *dellahs*, and applied it with a palette knife, allowing some of the original thin paint to show through. To vary this blue I added Ultramarine to the mix and the effect was quite vibrant. When using Texture Paste it is important to replace the cap immediately and clean off the palette knife. My next application of Texture Paste was tinted with Lemon Yellow and applied with an old soft brush to the highlights on the *dellahs*.

While the paste was drying, I painted the fruit and cloth with dilute Rowney Orange subdued with a little Payne's Grey. I could see all sorts of colours reflected in the *dellahs* and decided on an olive green as a basis, achieving this colour by mixing Rowney Orange with Monestial Blue. Then I emphasized the pattern on the cloth by darkening it with Payne's Grey.

Finished stage (fig. 108) You will have realized by now that I have used a very limited palette. It is sometimes a good idea to restrict yourself to a few colours, as this can give unity to a painting. This theme is continued in my choice of oil pastel colours, keeping to Orange, Payne's Grey and Lemon Yellow, but with the addition of Gold.

The colour on the *dellahs* has been warmed with thin washes of Rowney Orange, and dark tones added with Rowney Orange mixed with Payne's Grey. I also used Payne's Grey to make stripes on the small blue pot.

The cloth texture was a mixture of Orange, Yellow Ochre and a little Payne's Grey pastel freely applied. You cannot be too precise with such a broad, sticky medium. I used Gold oil pastel to give richness to the *dellahs*, scraping it back occasionally, and to soften the zigzag pattern on the cloth.

Fig. 107 **Second stage**

Fig. 108 **Finished stage, *Arabic Dellahs*, oil pastel and acrylic, 21.5 × 36 cm (8½ × 14¼ in)**

INDIAN INK AND ACRYLIC

Welsh Landscape I am finishing the book with another 'accidental' landscape. Although this is based on freely manipulated ink runs and wet-in-wet ink blots (**fig. 109**), I think it is a valid way of working. This unpredicted image had to be tamed and made to work for me. I believe it was Degas who said that a picture should not be just a copy, but the product of the imagination of the artist, to which natural elements could be added if desired.

In **fig. 110** I have used acrylic colour to add natural elements and create a Welsh landscape based on memories of white-washed cottages, narrow, winding, hilly roads and light patterns of fields. The ink blots became dark trees subdued with a semi-transparent film of acrylic, and precipitation in the ink represented scrubby foreground.

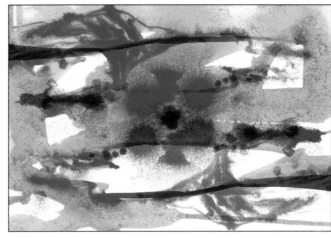

Fig. 109

Fig. 110 *Welsh Landscape*, Indian ink and acrylic, 21 × 29 cm (8¼ × 11½ in)